KU-175-403

Fencing

Produced in collaboration
with British Fencing

Produced for A & C Black by

Monkey Puzzle Media Ltd
Gissings Farm, Fressingfield
Suffolk IP21 5SH

Published in 2007 by

A & C Black Publishers Ltd
38 Soho Square, London W1D 3HB
www.acblack.com

Second edition 2007

ISBN: 978 0 7136 8375 2

A CIP record for this book is available from the
British Library.

Acknowledgements
Cover and inside design by James Winrow and
Tom Morris for Monkey Puzzle Media Ltd.
Cover photograph courtesy of Karina Hoskyns
Sports Photography (www.khsportsphotos.co.uk).
All other photographs in this publication courtesy
of Karina Hoskyns Sports Photography
(www.khsportsphotos.co.uk), except pages 6, 7
(excepting bottom-right), 9, 12–13, 15, 17, 19,
22–23, 27, 28–29, 30–31, 32, 34 (excepting top),
35 (excepting top- and bottom-left), 36, 38, 41
courtesy of Karina Hoskyns, page 55 top courtesy
of Empics (Adam Butler) and page 55 bottom
courtesy of Empics (Michael Sohn).
Illustrations by Dave Saunders, except page 52 by
Techtype.

KNOW THE GAME is a registered trademark.

Printed and bound in China by C&C Offset Printing
Co., Ltd.

Note: Throughout the book players and officials are
referred to as 'he'. This should, of course, be taken
to mean 'he or she' where appropriate. Similarly, all
instructions are geared towards right-handed players
– left-handers should simply reverse these instructions.

CONTENTS

FOREWORD

The modern sport of fencing has been included in every Olympic Games since Baron de Coubertin revived the ancient games in 1896. At the highest level, fencing is physically demanding, and requires intense concentration and tactical awareness. Fencers who may not reach these heights can regularly attend clubs and compete at regional and national levels.

GETTING INTO FENCING

Fencing is a great way of keeping fit without the risk of injury. The sport suits men, women and young people of all ages.

The sport appeals to those who may be reluctant to take part in team games. They enjoy the individuality of fencing, matching their skill, speed and intellect against those of an opponent.

Fencing challenges participants to perfect and perform disciplined movements, and study the theory and language of the sport for achievement awards.

Fencing is one of the few physical activities in which males and females take part on equal terms.

Fencing is like a game of chess, with attacks planned far in advance.

COMPETITIVE FENCING IN THE UK

British Fencing (BF) is the national governing body in the UK, and is responsible for selecting UK teams for World Championships and Olympic Games, as well as organising UK and international fencing events.

Each of the four home countries has its own organisation, which is represented on the BF Board. These are responsible for local development programmes, training of new coaches, club support and organising local competitions.

In the UK, there is a nationally organised series of championships at foil, épée and sabre for men, women and teams and these are open to all fencers throughout. Several international fencing events also take place in the UK and these attract fencers from all over the world.

Individual membership of BF through home country organisations is open to all new fencers, regardless of standard. Members regularly receive information on fencing events, *The Sword* magazine, notices and reports of competitions, and information from local organisers and clubs.

For more details, go to www.britishfencing.com. Alternatively, you can write to: General Secretary, British Fencing, 1 Barons Gate, 33–35 Rothschild Road, London W4 5HT.

Speed, tactics and timing are all important for success.

FENCING CONTACTS

To contact your home country association go to:

England
www.englandfencing.org.uk

Scotland
www.scottish-fencing.com

Wales
www.welshfencing.org

Northern Ireland
www.nifu.co.uk

INTRODUCTION

The sword is one of the oldest of weapons, and many types have been used in armed combat throughout the course of history. Traditional swords had heavy, broad blades, and required swordsman to have great strength as they were used to hack through adversaries, either on foot or on horseback.

SWORD DEVELOPMENT

As the use of armour developed as a means of protection, swords became larger and heavier, until two hands were required to wield the mighty weapons. However, following the invention of gunpowder, the musket and bayonet began to replace the sword for military use. Small swords continued to be carried by fashionable gentlemen for personal protection.

THE SALUTE

Fencing is a chivalrous sport, so it's customary to salute an opponent before a bout or competition. It is also courteous to salute your coach before and after receiving a lesson.

EXECUTING THE SALUTE

- Hold your mask under one arm and your sword in the other hand.
- Place your feet, heels touching, at right angles.
- Point the sword downwards in front of you.
- Raise the sword arm straight.
- Bring the sword to an upright position so that the guard is in line with your lips.
- Sweep the sword away, with the point downwards, to the original starting position.

The salute before crossing swords.

CLOTHING

Clothing for fencing is made to the highest standard and is designed to provide protection and mobility. Clothing can be any colour apart from black. Jackets for women have pockets for chest protectors, and these should always be used.

 Full chest protector.

Chest protectors.

A man, woman and child in full fencing kit. Jackets must overlap the breeches by at least 10cm at the waist. The breeches fasten under the knee and long socks cover the legs.

Masks must be adjusted to fit snugly.

An under-plastron is worn under the fencing jacket. This provides extra protection under the sword arm and to part of the chest and back.

One glove is worn on the sword hand. It has a long cuff that covers the jacket sleeve at least halfway between the wrist and the elbow.

WEAPONS

Three types of sword are used in fencing. These are the foil, the épée and the sabre. There are left- and right-handed versions, and smaller sizes are available for young participants.

THE FOIL

The foil is a light, flexible weapon, weighing 500g:

- the blade is rectangular or square in section, and must not be more than 90cm in length
- the overall length of the weapon must not exceed 110cm
- the point must be flattened and covered with a rubber or plastic button or, in the case of an electric foil, a sprung-metal point assembly
- the circular guard must pass through a gauge of 12cm diameter.

ELECTRIC HITS

Some foils have sprung metal points. These can be wired to electrical apparatus, which then measure whenever a hit is successful. To be successful, a hit must be made with at least 500g pressure.

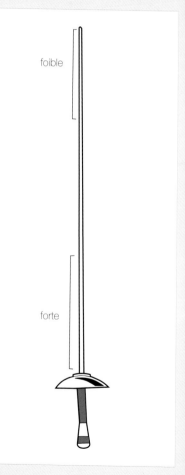

foible

forte

 The foil.

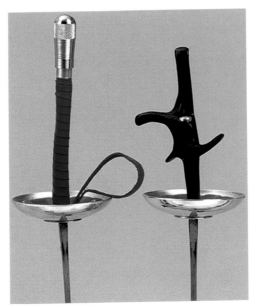

Foils – French grip (left) and pistol grip (right).

> **Thrusts with the point at the opponent's trunk count as valid hits.**

FOIL HANDLE

Different types of handle are commonly used:

- French/straight grip – handles are usually covered with leather or rubber
- orthopaedic/pistol grip – moulded handles with finger protrusions.

French grip

French-handle foils have a pommel, which acts as a counterbalance to the blade. A leather loop, known as a 'martingale', is fitted between the guard pad and the handle. The martingale is held in the fingers of the sword hand, and ensures that the foil is not wrenched from the fencer's hand during a bout.

Pistol grip

Orthopaedic handles, or 'pistol grips', are available in many designs. They are usually moulded in plastic or aluminium. They must not have attachments that protect the user, or protrusions that extend beyond the guard.

Pistol grips must not be designed in such a way as to allow the opponent's blade to become entangled in them. They do not normally require a martingale. They must comply with the maximum permitted length of the weapon.

THE ÉPÉE

The épée is based on the duelling rapier. It is heavier than the foil, weighing 770g.

- The blade has a triangular section. It is grooved and is the same length as the foil (90cm).

- It must have a protected point or sprung-metal point assembly.

- The guard, which protects the épée fencer's forearm, must have a maximum diameter of 13.5cm.

- The rules governing handles are the same as those for the foil.

Valid hits are scored by thrusting the point at any part of the opponent's body, arms, legs and head.

ELECTRIC HITS

Like foils, some épées can be wired into an electrical scoring system. The system measures hits with the point of the blade, which have to be delivered with 750g pressure to score.

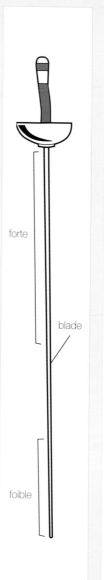

foible

blade

forte

blade

foible

forte

blade

 The épée.

 The sabre.

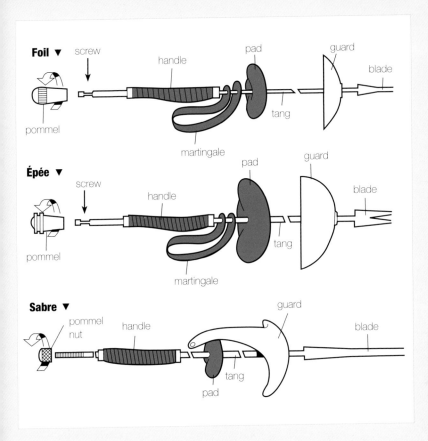

Foil ▼

screw
handle
pad
guard
blade
pommel
martingale
tang

Épée ▼

screw
handle
pad
guard
blade
pommel
martingale
tang

Sabre ▼

pommel nut
handle
guard
blade
tang
pad

THE SABRE

Weapon parts.

The sabre is a lighter, more flexible version of the military sabre. It is the same weight as the foil (500g).

- The total length must not exceed 105cm.

- The blade is rectangular in section.

- The guard is shaped to protect the sword hand and forearm, and it must pass through a gauge 15cm x 14cm.

Hits are scored by using edge 'cuts' or point thrusts. Hits scored on the opponent's body above the hips, arms and head count as valid.

BASIC MOVEMENTS

The basic position in fencing is the On Guard position. From this stance, the fencer is ready to move forwards and backwards, and to launch attacks against an opponent, for example the lunge and recovery. Many of the basic movements apply to foil, épée and sabre.

THE ON GUARD

The On Guard is the 'get ready' position. It enables the fencer to be balanced but also ready to change direction while continuing to threaten the opponent with the weapon.

ASSUMING THE ON GUARD POSITION

First, decide if you will hold the sword in the right or left hand. Make sure you have the correct version of your chosen sword and the correct clothing.

- Stand with your feet about hip-width apart, with the leading foot (sword-arm side) pointing towards the opponent and the rear foot at right angles, with both heels in line.

- Keep your body upright, with your weight equally distributed on both feet.

- Bend both knees, keeping the body upright and your weight evenly balanced.

- Your heels should still be in line; you should be looking in the direction of your leading foot.

- Lift your sword arm so it is directly over your leading leg, with the hand about chest-high.

- Slightly bend your elbow.

- Raise your non-sword arm in a relaxed position away from the body.

 Right-handed On Guard from the front.

TRAINING

Practise coming On Guard in one movement, preferably in front of a mirror, looking straight ahead.

It is very important that you are able to relax your shoulders and arms in the correct position, while keeping the body upright. Practise until you are able to assume the On Guard position without thinking how.

 Left-handed On Guard from the front.

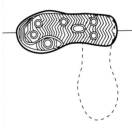

 Feet position for the right-handed On Guard. Keep the left foot still and pivot the right foot round on the heel until it is at right angles to the left.

The On Guard position is the same for both the foil and épée. For the sabre, the sword hand is much lower, usually about waist height. The non-sword arm is held low and well back to avoid this being hit.

MOVEMENT ON THE PISTE

Fencers compete on a piste that is 14m long and 2m wide. They can move forwards and backwards on the piste as necessary, but they are penalised if they leave the piste. Fencers are not allowed to pass each other to change sides while fencing.

When moving on the piste, fencers must try to maintain balance so that they can react to the opponent's movements. They must constantly be ready to take advantage of the opponent's mistakes.

Fencing steps are generally performed so that the distance between the front and rear feet is maintained. Unlike walking, the feet do not close up or cross, as this would result in a loss of balance.

Practise the techniques for moving forward and back. Keep the basics in mind, but don't dwell on them too much or your movements will become stiff and jerky.

Once in a while, use a cross step or a short run to gain a tactical surprise. Remember, you will be at a disadvantage if the surprise move fails!

Remember not to close your feet together.

MOVING FORWARDS

Moving forwards without crossing your feet, or even getting them too close together, takes practice.

- The front foot is moved forwards, just clearing the ground, with the heel contacting the ground first. The rear foot, keeping equal distance, moves forwards with the toe contacting the ground first.

- Balance is maintained by keeping the weight between the feet and moving from the knee and not the hip.

- The heels are kept in line with each other and the knees stay bent throughout the step.

MOVING BACKWARDS

Stepping backwards uses a reverse technique from stepping forwards.

- The rear foot, just clearing the ground, is moved backwards. The toe makes contact with the ground first. The front foot, keeping equal distance, moves backwards with the heel contacting the ground first.

Steps forward begin by moving the leading foot. After each step, the fencer must be On Guard.

LUNGE AND RECOVERY

When lunging, your sword must cover the distance between you and your opponent's target area as quickly as possible. At the same time, your target must be protected.

Balance must be maintained at maximum lunge so that you have the option of returning to On Guard, fencing from the lunge position, or recovering forward to press home an advantage.

THE LUNGE

These are the key elements of the lunge technique. Aim to extend your arm slowly and smoothly, and try to make the effort come from the elbow – do not punch from the shoulder.

- Your hand should finish in line with the shoulder, with the thumb on top of the sword.

- As your arm is straightening, raise the front foot from the ground toe first (almost the same action as the step forwards) and kick forward by straightening the back leg with the back foot flat on the floor.

- Your front foot should land heel first with the leading knee vertically over the heel of the front foot.

- Your rear arm should be thrown back.

The fencer on the right executes the lunge. Notice how the back leg is straight and the rear arm is thrown back.

POINTS TO CHECK ON THE LUNGE

- Back foot flat on the ground.
- Back knee straight.
- Sword arm straight and shoulder-high.
- Leading knee vertically above leading heel.
- Rear arm thrown back.
- Head and body upright.

When you practise the lunge, increase the drive as the back leg is straightened, making each lunge faster.

THE RECOVERY

The lunge and recovery are usually executed as one movement.

- As your heel hits the ground during the lunge, use the rebound action to carry your front foot backwards.

- At the same time, bend the back knee and lift the back arm.

- When the front heel touches the ground again, bend your sword arm.

You should be back in the On Guard position, perfectly balanced, and ready to move backwards or forwards, or to attack again.

The lunge and recovery. The sword arm must begin straightening first. Kick forwards with the front foot and push with the back leg until it is straight. Recovery to the On Guard begins by bending the rear leg.

FLÈCHE

The flèche is an alternative way of reaching the target at foil and épée. It is a much more tactical offensive action, and must be executed at the correct time and distance from the opponent.

- As you straighten your arm, shift your centre of gravity forwards, rapidly tipping your body towards the horizontal but trying to keep the front knee bent for as long as possible.

- Your back foot should swing past the front foot to stop loss of balance.

- As your back foot leaves the ground and starts to swing past the front foot, push off from the front foot, propelling yourself quickly and powerfully forwards.

- Both feet leave the ground for a fraction of a second, as your body is near horizontal.

The hit must arrive on the target before your back foot touches the ground.

The fencer on the right has executed the flèche. Note the position of the rear arm.

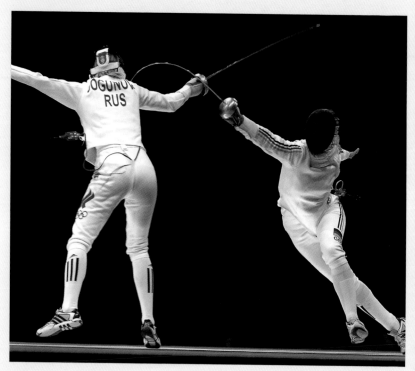

The balestra is a short, sharp jump forwards.

BALESTRA

The balestra is a short, sharp jump forwards, used to surprise the opponent before making an attack, or used to draw the opponent's attack.

The action is similar to a step forwards, but as you lift your front foot, jump forwards sharply from the rear foot and land on both feet at the same time.

LIKE AN ARROW

'Flèche' is the French word for arrow, and this perfectly describes the movement – the point leads and the rest of the body follows as near horizontally as possible.

FENCING WITH THE FOIL

In fencing with the foil, valid hits are scored by thrusting the foil point at the opponent's trunk. Hits on the arms, legs or head do not count as valid and are considered 'off target'. A valid hit must be made with enough force to slightly bend the foil blade – if the point were sharp, it would pierce the flesh.

MAKING AN ATTACK

During a bout either fencer may choose to attack. An attack is defined in the rules as an offensive action made by a fencer who is extending the sword arm and is directing his or her foil point towards the opponent's trunk.

An attack is a reach forwards to hit one's opponent on the body with the foil point.

▼ A fencing bout is a test of concentration, tactical awareness, explosive actions and immediate reactions.

ATTACK AND DEFENCE

If a fencer chooses to attack his or her opponent during a bout, the opponent must recognise this as a valid attempt to score a hit, and must try to defend by deflecting the oncoming point with their own foil. Alternatively they must completely avoid the attack by a movement of the body or feet.

If the defender successfully deflects the attacking blade, they may immediately hit back and the attacker must defend.

REACTION

Sometimes the opponent is surprised by an attack and reacts by hitting back without first deflecting the oncoming point. In this case, the attacking fencer will be awarded the hit even if both hits are simultaneous, provided the attack hits the valid target. Defenders must always parry an attack before scoring points of their own.

FENCING PHRASE

The exchange of alternatively hitting and defending, or phrase, occurs each time either fencer chooses to attack. It continues until one fencer makes a hit, either valid or off target, or until the exchange is broken off.

PARRY AND RIPOSTE

The action of defending is known as parrying, and hitting back following a successful parry is known as riposting. Experienced fencers are trained to execute a variety of attacks to deceive their opponent's attempts to parry and riposte.

During a bout, both fencers will try to create a moment when they catch the opponent off guard in order to deliver a successful attack. At the same time, they must remain aware of a possible attack, and be ready to parry and riposte.

Flexibility and fast reactions are key if you want to avoid quick attacks.

HOLDING THE FOIL

When the foil is held correctly, it is possible to place the point to the opponent's target with enough accuracy and sufficient pressure to make the blade bend, but without using excessive force.

FRENCH GRIP

Place the thumb of your sword hand close to the pad, laying it flat on the top edge of the foil handle, and curl your index finger around underneath.

- The last three fingers of the sword hand should rest on the handle, pressing the pommel lightly into the wrist.
- When the sword arm is bent at the elbow, a straight line must be formed between the elbow and the point of the foil, the foil forming an extension of the sword arm.

HITTING

The correct method of hitting is designed to ensure the greatest chance of scoring on the opponent's target. This is not easy when moving at speed.

Foil fencers must be able to hit the opponent on target while at short, medium or long distance. Short-distance hitting may be necessary while performing a riposte. It may also be necessary when performing a renewal of attack or riposte where the opponent has attempted to avoid the initial action.

THE FOIL TARGET

The target is the trunk of the body from the top of the neck down to a 'V' at the groin, from the hips at the front and down to a horizontal line across the hip bones at the back and sides.

The French grip. The two central fingers pass through the martingale.

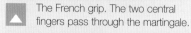

The pistol grip. This is held in the same way as the French grip, but the fingers fit into the mouldings.

Angle the blade to hit areas of the target other than the chest – the back or flanks. This may involve rotating the sword hand or hitting with a bent arm.

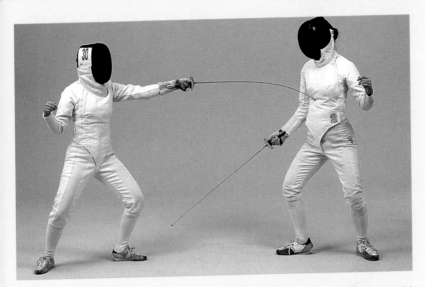

The hit is made by lowering the point while extending the sword arm. The blade must bend slightly, and the sword hand and shoulder should be relaxed.

The foil target is the dotted area in this photo. The arms below the seams of the sleeves joining the body of the jacket and the bib of the mask, which partly covers the neck and chest, are off target.

MEDIUM- AND LONG-RANGE ATTACKS

Attacks at medium distance are normally performed with a lunge or flèche, with the sword arm fully extended. Long-distance attacks usually involve combinations of footwork, step lunge or step flèche. The opponent may attempt to avoid being hit by stepping in close and the attacker must be able to respond to this with a close renewal.

ON GUARD

When On Guard, the foil is held in a position that threatens the opponent's target but also limits the opponent's choice of target to attack. The foil target is identified in four areas or 'lines'. A theoretical horizontal line is drawn midway across the trunk of the body, producing high lines and low lines.

The left-hand and right-hand areas depend on the position of the sword hand.

When On Guard with the foil in line with the sword-arm shoulder, it will only be possible for the opponent to attack the high-line target along one side of the blade, the inside open line. Attacking on the opposite side of the blade, the outside closed line, will completely miss the target.

The fencer who is correctly On Guard and is confident that the opponent cannot attack in the closed line will have to try to assess when the opponent will attack, and not where.

To protect the open line, the fencer must move the blade across his or her body to a position close to the opposite extremity of their own target while still threatening the opponent's target. However, this will open the sword-arm side line.

HITTING PRACTICE

Start by hitting a stationary target, for example a wall pad or a willing partner who is fully kitted.

- Stand at a distance where you can hit by just extending your sword arm.
- Push with your thumb and lower the foil point while extending your arm.
- Tighten your grip as the blade bends, and hold the hit on the target.
- Try to keep your shoulder relaxed all the time, and avoid 'punching' the hit.
- You should practise hitting at different distances, with a bent arm, with a fully extended arm, or while lunging.

Close distance hitting.

GUARDS

There are four high-line guards, and four low-line guards, and these are numbered as in the original French School of Fencing. The four main guards, two high- and two low-line, are made with the sword hand in a semi-supinated position (thumb uppermost). In the four alternative guards, the sword hand is rotated into a pronated position (knuckles uppermost).

Sixte. A semi-supinated high-line guard on the sword-arm side. The sword hand is in line with the elbow and shoulder, and the foil blade slopes upwards to continue the line of the forearm.

Quarte. A high-line guard with the sword hand in semi-supination on the non-sword arm side or opposite side of the target to sixte. When moving the foil across the body to form this guard, bend the wrist so that the foil point continues to threaten the opponent. The blade should finish in a position parallel to the position in sixte.

Septime. The hand should be in the same position as for quarte, but the foil blade is angled down to protect the low line on the non-sword arm side of the target. The foil point must be at a height where it should hit the opponent in the low line when the sword arm is extended without any correction of the blade.

Octave. The hand should be as for sixte, semi-supinated on the sword-arm side, but with the foil blade angled down to protect the low line. The foil point should hit the opponent's low line with an extension of the sword arm without correction of the blade.

PRACTISING GUARDS

- Adopt each guard in turn while standing in front of a mirror and check if you can see any exposed target in the outside line.
- With a training partner, check each other's guards by attacking into the outside lines.

In the correct guard position, you should be ready both to attack and to defend, and ready to score a hit by extending the sword arm.

 Sixte.

Quarte.

 Septime.

Octave.

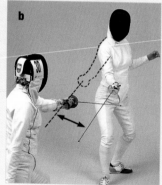

Lateral parry.

PARRIES

When defending against an opponent's attack, it is necessary to oppose and deflect the oncoming foible with your own forte (see pages 8 and 11). To enable you to score immediately with a riposte, it is essential that your parry finishes in the correct guard.

The direction in which the attacking blade travels determines the nature of the parry. Parries are identified by the movement of the point and the guard in which they finish.

Lateral parry (also known as a simple parry). The blade is moved laterally across the target, either in the high line or low line. In the high line this is from sixte to quarte or vice versa (a), and from octave to septime or vice versa in the low line (b).

Circular parry of sixte (c) and quarte (d). The point of the foil is moved in a circular path to collect the oncoming attacking blade and carry this into the outside line. The parry starts and finishes in the same guard. It is important to consider the direction of rotation and ensure that the defending blade passes under the attacking blade in the high line and over the attacking blade in the low line.

Semicircular parry from sixte to octave (e) and from quarte to septime (f). The parry is made by moving the foil point in a semicircular path from the high line to the low line on the same side of the target, or vice versa.

Diagonal parry from sixte to septime (g) and from quarte to octave (h). Similar to a semicircular parry but the foil is moved diagonally across the target from high line to low line, or vice versa.

Circular parry.

Semicircular parry.

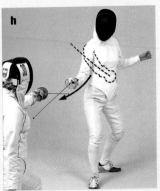

Diagonal parry.

SIMPLE ATTACKS

The object of making a simple attack is to score a hit on your opponent's valid target either by attacking into the open line (direct attack) or by an indirect attack that passes over (cut-over) or under (disengage) your opponent's blade.

Attacks can be made with a lunge or flèche. Indirect attacks must be made with the minimum of movement, and the foil must be manipulated using the thumb and forefinger of the sword hand.

Straight thrust: a direct attack into the open line. It is not necessary to pass over or under the opponent's blade.

> **Before making an attack, reconnoitre and study your opponent's defence. Then make your attack accordingly.**

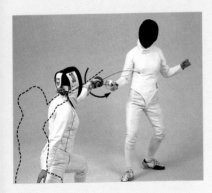

Disengage: an indirect attack that passes under the opponent's blade.

Cut-over: an indirect attack that passes over the opponent's blade.

COMPOUND ATTACKS

Compound attacks are two or more simple attacks executed in succession. The first simple attack is made as a feint or false attack to draw the opponent's parry.

The subsequent movements of the attack deceive the parry to deliver the hit.

Simple parries are deceived with one-twos; circular parries are deceived with a double; and semicircular parries with low-high compound attacks.

PREPARATION

To create a situation in which an attack can be made during a bout, start with a preparation. This may be a fast step forwards or balestra, before the lunge or flèche. This will allow you to get closer and surprise the opponent, or cause the two foil blades to come into contact (known as engagement). This can be either a pressure or a beat, which is a sharp strike of the opponent's blade.

DEFENCE ON THE LUNGE

Having made an attack with a lunge that has been successfully parried by the opponent, the attacker must defend against the immediate riposte. There will be no time to recover from the lunge, so the parry and counter-riposte must be made from the lunge position.

A successful preparation can have the effect of making the opponent momentarily 'freeze' or over-react.

FENCING WITH THE ÉPÉE

The rules governing foil fencing – termed 'conventions' – do not apply to épée. Because the whole body, including arms, legs and head, is a valid target, épée theory is based on scoring a hit without being hit yourself (just as it would be in a duel with sharp swords!).

ÉPÉE TECHNIQUE

The épéeist is trained to react to an oncoming attack from the opponent by counterattacking, usually to the attacking fencer's sword arm. This is done either by angulating the épée to avoid the attack, or by engaging and holding the opponent's blade, in opposition, while scoring a hit.

It is also a common technique to use renewals – additional attempts to hit – following an initial attack or counterattack.

Many of the actions that are used at foil are also used by the épéeist. However, more care is taken by the épéeist not to expose his or her sword arm to attacks and counterattacks.

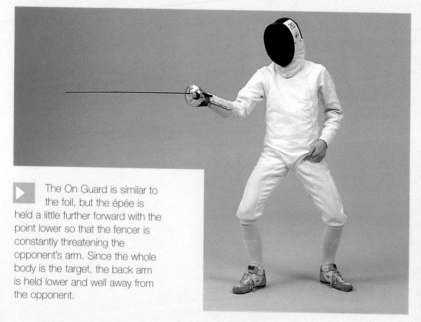

The On Guard is similar to the foil, but the épée is held a little further forward with the point lower so that the fencer is constantly threatening the opponent's arm. Since the whole body is the target, the back arm is held lower and well away from the opponent.

Attack and counterattack at épée. Unlike the situation in a duel, épée fencers have to score a number of valid hits to win a bout. If both hit each other within a twenty-fifth of a second, both score a hit.

KEEP YOUR DISTANCE

A keen awareness of distance is necessary to avoid being taken by surprise by a direct attack to the body, leg or foot. Épéeists usually stay further away from the opponent than foilists, so that attacks to the body require a step lunge.

ATTACKS

Direct attack (to leg). Attacks to the lower body have the risk of exposing the attacker's upper body to counterattack. Therefore, these must be made very fast and with the element of surprise.

Attack with opposition (body). When fencing an opponent who constantly counterattacks, control their blade while attempting to score a hit. A tactic to achieve this is to draw the counterattack by making a false attack, usually to the opponent's arm. The attacker then takes the opponent's blade with his or her own blade – prise de fer – and continues the attack while maintaining contact with his or her blade.

COUNTERATTACKS

Counterattack with angulation. Try to avoid the opponent's point while making a counterattack by angling the blade. Angulation is also necessary to hit the opponent's sword hand and wrist, as these are hidden behind the large guard of the épée.

Counterattack with opposition. Where it is not possible to avoid the opponent's attack and score with a counterattack, it is necessary to counterattack while maintaining contact with the opponent's blade.

Parry riposte. Although the initial reaction of the épéeist is to counterattack an attacker, it may be necessary to parry and riposte if the counterattack fails or the attack is well timed and made with a long lunge or flèche.

STEPPING BACK

Combining an angulated counterattack with a step back provides two opportunities to score:

- the counterattack itself

- a parry riposte if the counterattack fails.

FENCING WITH THE SABRE

In fencing with the sabre, it is necessary to defend the trunk of the body above the hips, head and arms against hits with both the point and edge cuts. This requires the sabre to be held in a different way to that at foil and épée.

SABRE TECHNIQUE

The conventions at sabre are the same as those at foil, so it is necessary to parry the opponent's attack before gaining the right to riposte. As defensive movements are large and easily deceived, defence with distance (in which the defending fencer moves back) while trying to access and close the attacker's final line, is a primary tactic.

This is often anticipated by the attacker, who will precede the attack with a preparation of one or more steps before attacking with a lunge.

This, in turn, presents an opportunity for the sabreur who is moving away to attack into the opponent's preparation:

- with a cut to the opponent's sword arm
- by maintaining an extended sword arm with the point in line with the oncoming target.

HOLDING THE SABRE

Hold the sabre with the blade in a near vertical position with the point slightly ahead of the hand.

- Place the thumb of your sword hand on the back of the handle with your index finger on the opposite side. The thumb and finger pinch the handle.
- The handle rests in the base of the remaining fingers so that the pommel nut protrudes below your hand.

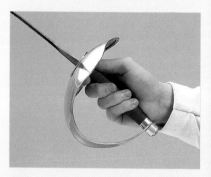

The sabre grip enables the sword to be steadied by the palm of the hand and manipulated by turning the hand from supination (palm uppermost) to pronation (knuckles uppermost).

SABRE ATTACK AND DEFENCE

At sabre, the sword arm and hand form part of the target area, and are vulnerable to attack and counterattack.

- Fencers normally keep a distance that means a lunge is required to score a hit on the hand or arm.

- Lunges provide the chance to make a counterattack on the attacker's sword arm.

- If the counterattack fails, it can be followed up with a parry riposte.

It is necessary to defend against point thrusts and edge cuts. The latter may be delivered laterally to either side of the body or vertically to the head and arm.

At sabre, lateral cuts to the head are known as 'cheek cuts'.

HITTING

A sabre cut is made by extending the sword arm and presenting the edge of the blade to the intended target.

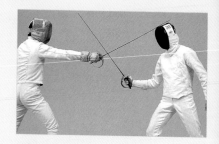

 Cut to the head.

- The thumb and index finger act as a fulcrum as the remaining fingers pull the handle into the palm. This causes the blade to swing forward so that it makes contact and rebounds, delivering a crisp cut.

- Point hits are made by fully extending the sword arm while holding the sabre with the hand in full pronation.

- The sword arm should be about shoulder high, with the point of the sabre slightly lower so that the blade bends correctly on impact.

- Cuts to the head are made with the hand in semi-supination.

Cut to the chest: chest cuts are made with the hand in supination with fencers of the same hand, or in pronation with opposite-hand fencers.

Cut to the flank: when both fencers are right-handed or both are left-handed, flank cuts are made with the hand in pronation. With opposite-hand fencers, flank cuts are made with the hand in supination. The extended sword arm should be lower than shoulder height.

 Point to line.

THE TARGET

The target at sabre is defined as any part of the body above a horizontal line drawn between the top of the folds formed by the thighs and the trunk of the fencer when in the On Guard position.

The sword arm is vulnerable to short attacks made by the opponent with a lunge and counter-attacks delivered by the opponent who is moving backwards.

 A lamé jacket and mask cover the sabre target area for electric scoring apparatus.

GUARDS

There are five sabre guards to defend the target against lateral cuts to the flank and chest and vertical cuts to the head. They are numbered as in the original French School of Fencing.

Prime. The guard of prime protects the chest and lower target on the non-sword arm side against lateral cuts. The hand is held in pronation at head height with the sabre blade pointing downwards and the point slightly forward. The cutting edge should meet the attacking blade.

Seconde. Seconde protects the flank and lower target on the sword arm side, and the hand is in pronation with the blade pointing down. The hand is normally held slightly lower than in the guard of prime and the blade turned outward so that the cutting edge meets the attacking blade.

Tierce. The hand is semi-supinated in tierce with the blade held in the near vertical with the point slightly forward. The cutting edge is turned to meet lateral cuts to the flank and head. The hand should be in line with the lower limit of the target area.

Quarte. The guard of quarte protects the chest and head against lateral cuts and is similar to the position of tierce but on the opposite side of the target.

Quinte. The head is protected against vertical cuts with the guard of quinte. The sabre is raised above the head with the sword arm bent at the elbow and the forearm vertical. The sword hand should be in pronation with the blade across the head and the point should be slightly forward and higher than the hand. The blade is held so that the cutting edge opposes the attacking blade.

PARRIES AND RIPOSTES

The choice of guards to perform parries depends largely on the target selected by the opponent for the attack.

- The opponent may make a false attack to one area to draw the parry then change direction to another area to deceive the parry.

- The sabreur must be skilled in moving quickly from one guard to another to perform successive parries.

- The selection of target for hitting with a riposte is the same as those for the attack. Therefore a parry to any guard can be followed by a riposte to head, chest or flank.

All guards can be used to defend against point attacks.

 Prime.

 Seconde.

 Tierce.

 Quarte.

Quinte.

PRACTISING GUARDS

- Check guards in front of a mirror and practise moving quickly from one guard to another.
- Defend against attacks to various targets made by a training partner.
- Develop phrases using different guards with a training partner.

FENCING ON A PISTE

Organised bouts and matches are conducted on a piste. This is 14m long and 2m wide. There are two On Guard lines marked 2m either side of the centre line. Lines are marked 2m in from either end, and these sections are shaded. The shaded sections indicate to the fencers that they are approaching the rear limits. Either fencer may move forwards or backwards as necessary, but they may not cross the boundaries of the piste, or change ends while fencing.

AT THE START

After the fencers have saluted and put on their masks, the referee gives the instruction to come On Guard and asks if both fencers are ready. If they are both ready, the referee says 'Play'.

The bout continues until the referee gives the instruction to 'Halt'. Both fencers must stop immediately and maintain their positions on the piste until the referee has either awarded a hit or restarted the bout.

RESTART

After each valid hit is awarded, both fencers must resume their positions in the centre of the piste behind their respective On Guard lines.

> Before the bout begins, both fencers must be behind their respective On Guard lines.

▶ Fencing on a piste requires excellent balance.

RULES ON PISTE

- If either fencer is forced back to a position where both feet cross the rear limit line, the referee calls 'Halt' and the opponent is awarded a hit.
- The referee also calls 'Halt' when a fencer crosses the side lines with one foot. The fencers are replaced On Guard on the piste, and the bout is restarted.
- A fencer who crosses a side line with both feet is penalised by having to move back 1m before the bout is restarted.
- Fencers cannot score a valid hit when they have both feet off the piste.
- If there is a simultaneous hit by both fencers, and one fencer is off the piste, even with only one foot, the fencer who is still on the piste will score.

Fencers on a piste, seen from overhead.

TACTICS

In competitive fencing, selection of the correct stroke must be combined with the ability to execute it at the right time and distance. Coordination of mind and body is crucial. Try and develop confidence in your ability to make the right moves when you are fencing. Self-confidence helps to relieve stress and allows you to relax and achieve the required coordination.

ASSESSING YOUR OPPONENT

The form of attack is generally dictated by your opponent's defensive actions. If his or her defensive movements are of a circular nature, your attacks must also be circular in order to deceive and hit.

MIX IT UP

A conscious effort must be made to vary your own game because your opponent will, of course, be trying to anticipate your next move by noting your habits. You can counter-bluff by reacting to exploratory moves in a way that encourages him or her to use a particular stroke, which you may turn to your advantage.

TIMING

Attacks and ripostes, however well chosen, will often fail unless they are delivered at the right moment and at the right speed. For example, a disengage should be timed as the opponent's blade is moving away from the line in which you intend to hit him or her, not while it is moving close to that line.

It is equally important to adjust the speed of a stroke to that of the opponent's timing and rhythm. For example, a one-two may fail because it is made so fast that the slower-reacting opponent will not respond to the feint, and his or her blade will not have moved away from the original line of engagement.

Develop timing by training with a partner who moves their blade back and forth between two guards in a rhythm, while you practise deceiving their blade with your own.

WATCHING YOUR OPPONENT

Most fencers have favourite strokes or actions. You can discover which your opponent favours by watching their response or feeling those movements through your blade – sentiment du fer. This tactical approach may be applied in the early stages of a bout by reconnaissance actions, feints, simple attacks and false attacks.

Launch an attack as your opponent is preparing to attack, when he or she is momentarily less vigilant in defence.

Try to anticipate your opponent's reaction when you launch an attack.

CADENCE

An opponent's speed, or cadence, can be determined during the initial exploratory moves mentioned above. It is often possible to impose your own cadence during a bout by varying the speed of movement. A sudden speeding up of the final movement or a broken time attack may achieve success.

The boxing saying, 'Box a fighter, fight a boxer' applies just as well to fencing. Attack an attacker but not a fencer who relies on defence to score hits.

 The unorthodox often works!

When fencing at close quarters, be aware that mistakes can cause offences, and offences are subject to penalties.

WATCH THE SPACE

A sense of distance must be developed by practice. Changes of distance by stepping forwards or back can be used tactically to make it more difficult for opponents to time attacks or preparations.

IN CLOSE

Fencing at close quarters is often effective at foil with sufficient blade control. It is less safe at épée and sabre. At close quarters at épée, try to force the corps à corps, without violence or to avoid being hit. These are offences, subject to penalty under the rules.

TACTICAL TIPS

- Confuse the counter-attacker so that he or she either misses or hits out of time.
- When fencing an opponent with a long reach who continually renews his or her attack, shorten the distance by stepping forwards into the attack. This gives the opponent less room to manoeuvre.
- Against a fencer who will not give the blade, false attacks or well-marked feints can be used to draw his or her reaction.
- If this is a counterattack, meet it with a counter-time, preferably taking the blade.
- If he or she makes a parry, a composed attack or a counter-riposte may score.
- If he or she returns to engagement, an appropriate attack can be made.
- When fencing an opponent who habitually attacks into the attack, draw his or her attack prematurely by using a false attack with a half lunge, or by a change of measure to score with attacks on the blade or ripostes.

THE FLÈCHE ATTACK

- This is especially effective at épée and foil.

- It can be used as a riposte against an opponent who makes a rapid recovery after being parried.

- It is also used to conclude a second intention attack.

FALL BACK

When it is hard to analyse an opponent's game, it is best to increase your distance. This will give you more time to study his or her methods by forcing longer preparations for attacks.

GROUNDWORK

- Use the piste tactically.

- Do not waste ground by retiring unnecessarily.

- Take every opportunity to regain ground lost during a bout.

- Forcing a defensive fencer back on to the rear line may induce him or her to attack.

- If you are superior in defence, the opponent may be forced to attack by falling back to your rear line.

 Increased distance will force your opponent to make big preparations.

Left-handers are vulnerable to attack at flank.

LEFTIES

Left-handers are often vulnerable to attacks or ripostes which end in the low lines, particularly at flank. Feints into octave sometimes encourage left-handers to leave the quarte or high lines open to attack.

It is possible to disconcert a faster opponent and regain the initiative by making changes of engagement in varying tempo.

BOUNCING FOOTWORK

Being able to move on the piste, make rapid changes of direction and launch sudden attacks is crucial for success.

- Fencers often use a bouncing form of footwork, continually bouncing on their toes.

- This lets them make small adjustments to distance, constantly reacting to their opponent's movement.

WHEELCHAIR FENCING

Organised wheelchair fencing began at Stoke Mandeville Hospital in 1953. It now enjoys national and international status with a full calendar of events including European, World and Paralympic championships. In the UK, wheelchair fencing is organised by the British Disabled Fencing Association (BDFA), which is affiliated to British Fencing (BF).

COMPETITIVE WHEELCHAIR FENCING

Wheelchair fencing is static, and in competitions, wheelchairs are clamped to frames on the floor to stop them from falling over.

- Two right-handed or two left-handed fencers face in opposite directions.
- The frames are adjusted to achieve the correct distance between the fencers, depending upon their reach and the weapon involved.
- When the fencers are of opposite hand, then they face the same way.
- Both fencers may lean forwards and backwards to attack and defend but they must remain in contact with the chair seat.
- They may stabilise themselves by holding the chair with the non-sword hand but must keep their feet on the chair footrest.

TRAINING

- When training in a club where frames are not available, the fencer's chairs are held in place by volunteers holding the wheels.
- Able-bodied fencers can sit in an ordinary chair to fence a wheelchair fencer. They must follow the rules for wheelchair fencing.
- Coaches conduct training exercises working on a one-to-one basis in which both coach and fencer are seated.

RULES FOR COMPETITION

These are the main differences and additions to the rules of fencing for disabled competitors:

- The target for foil and sabre is the same as for able-bodied fencing. At épée only hits above the waist count as valid.

- Chairs are covered with a metal lamé apron for épée and hits on the chair do not register.

- The distance between fencers is determined by one fencer fully extending his or her sword arm while sitting straight and touching the opponent's bent sword arm with the sword point. The opponent holds his or her sword vertically.

- At foil the point must touch the inside of the bent elbow joint. At épée and sabre the point must touch the external point of the elbow joint.

- The fencer with the shortest arm may choose to fence at his or her distance or the longer distance determined by the opponent's reach.

- Distance is adjusted by altering the frames. These are locked into position.

▼ Disability sport is usually organised in categories of abilities. In fencing, those with leg amputations normally fence from a wheelchair, even if they do not normally require one.

TRAINING

Fencing cannot be learned thoroughly unless you start by joining a class at a local club. The coach will explain and demonstrate elementary skills. You will be able to practise these with your class colleagues, and see how they fit into the overall game. Keeping fit by exercising in other ways will improve your fencing. Above all, it's important that you do warm-up and warm-down exercises before and after training sessions.

WARMING UP

Make sure you are properly warmed up before you begin a training session. This is essential if you want to avoid injury, as fencing requires a flexible body. Before stretching, you should increase your heart rate by jogging, skipping or by playing a simple game. This increases the flow of blood to muscle tissue, which provides energy.

> **Leg stretches are very important, as much of the physical effort of fencing is carried out by this area of the body.**

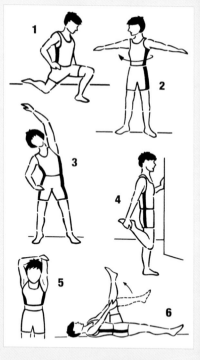

Examples of possible stretches you can do in your warm-up:
1) hip flexor stretch; **2)** trunk twist;
3) side stretch; **4)** quad stretch;
5) shoulder stretch; **6)** hamstring stretch.

STRETCHING

Stretching exercises are important as many of the common fencing positions can be difficult if you're not warmed up properly. Stretches should be specific and limited to the muscles that control movement in the shoulders, trunk and hips.

ROPE SKIPPING

The use of a skipping rope is not limited to warm-up. It helps to develop endurance and coordination that will lead to better mobility on the piste. It also has the advantage of being able to train alone and can be done in a limited area.

- Start by skipping with both feet together and develop a constant rhythm with two bounces per rotation.

- To begin with, you should be able to skip for a few minutes without stopping. Slowly increase the duration until you can keep going for about 20 minutes.

- As your skill improves try two bounces on alternate feet per rotation, keeping a constant rhythm.

INJURY

Make sure your fitness and training programme is balanced and regular. The coach at your club can help with this. Over-training for short periods of time followed by long periods of less or no training will result in injury.

FIGHTING FIT

- Specific group footwork training will help to develop mobility.
- Individual lessons with the coach will improve technical skills and tactical knowledge.
- Competitive training in the form of 'theme' fencing exercises and training competitions are useful for monitoring improvement.
- Regular fencing training will develop overall endurance, flexibility and coordination.
- Fencers who compete on a regular basis will learn how to plan their training to fit in with their competition programme, and to set primary and intermediate goals.

When skipping, look straight ahead and not at your feet.

COMPETITIVE FENCING

The Fédération Internationale d'Escrime (FIE) is the international governing body of fencing. The system of competition organisation used for the World Championships and World Cup events is determined by FIE, which also organises fencing at the Olympic Games under the direction of the International Olympic Committee (IOC). National Governing Bodies of Fencing organise their own major championships in line with the FIE rules.

MAJOR TOURNAMENTS

Competitions take the form of a knockout system in which fencers are seeded into a first-round poule according to their world ranking. They compete against the other fencers in their poule, normally five or six, for the best of nine hits.

- The most successful fencers in the first round are promoted to a direct elimination tableau where, according to their first-round seeding, they each fence one opponent for the best of 15 hits.

- The winners are then promoted to the next level where they again fence another winner.

- This continues until four fencers are left in the competition and they fence for Gold, Silver and two Bronze medals.

REFEREEING

Club matches may use judges in addition to a referee to watch both fencers and to indicate, by raising their hands, when the fencers have been hit on or off target.

- Two judges stand either side of the piste at one end, and both watch the fencer on the opposite end. Two judges are similarly positioned at the opposite end of the piste to watch the other fencer.
- The referee occupies the area between both sets of judges in such a way that he or she has a clear view of all four judges and both fencers.

The referee stands so that he has a clear view of both fencers and all four judges.

US fencer Ivan Lee during the men's individual sabre round, Athens Olympics, 2004. He wears an electronic helmet, which lights up to indicate when a point has been scored.

ELECTRICAL RECORDING

Electrical recording apparatus for registering hits on or off target is used in competition fencing.

- For foil and sabre, each fencer wears a metallic lamé jacket that covers the target area. Competitors use special weapons that are wired to a recording box through a spool with a retractable lead.
- When a hit is made on target, a coloured light shows on the recording box and a buzzer sounds. A red light shows for one fencer, a green light for his or her opponent.
- At foil, white lights indicate off-target hits.
- Metallic jackets are not necessary for épée because the whole body is a valid target.
- The referee controls the bout, using the lights on the recording box to determine valid hits.

GLOSSARY

Angulation Creating an angle between the weapon and the sword arm by flexing the wrist and turning the sword hand palm-up and palm-down (supinating and pronating).

Annulment of hit A valid hit which is disallowed because of an infringement of the rules or a technical fault.

Attack An initial offensive action made by extending the sword arm and continuously threatening the opponent's target.

Back edge The edge of a sabre blade opposite to that of the cutting edge.

Barrage A fight-off to determine a result in the event of a tie.

Broken time When a pause is introduced into an action which is normally performed in one movement.

Close quarters When two fencers are close together but can still wield their weapons.

Compound actions Two or more single actions performed together as one continuous action.

Corps à corps Bodily contact between two fencers in a bout.

Cut A hit at sabre made by striking with the edge of the blade.

Cut-over (coupé) An indirect action made by passing the blade over the opponent's point.

Detachment When both blades break contact.

Direct Actions made without passing the blade under or over the opponent's blade.

Disciplinary code By taking part in a fencing competition, fencers 'pledge their honour' to observe the rules for competitions and the decisions of judges, and to be respectful towards the president and the members of the jury.

Double action When both fencers choose exactly the same moment to make an offensive action.

Elbow guard A pad worn on the fencer's sword-arm elbow for protection.

False actions Actions made to assess the opponent's reaction or to provoke a reaction which can be exploited.

Feint A threatening movement of the blade made with the intention of provoking a parry or similar response.

Fencing line When fencers are fencing each other, it should be possible to draw a theoretical straight line running through both leading feet and rear heels.

Fencing measure The distance between two fencers such that they must lunge fully to score a valid hit.

Fencing time The time required to perform one simple fencing action.

Flank The side of the trunk of the body on the sword-arm side.

Hit To strike the opponent with the point of the sword clearly and distinctly and with character of penetration. A cut with a sabre.

Jury The president and judges who officiate during a bout.

Jury d'appel During a competition, a fencer or team captain may ask for a jury d'appel to be convened if he or she believes a misapplication of the rules has occurred. The jury will consist of one representative of each competing nation, or members of the organising committee.

Lines Theoretical divisions of the target, corresponding to fencing guards.

Lunge A method of getting closer to an opponent with acceleration to make an attack, and while maintaining balance and making it possible for a rapid recovery to On Guard.

One-two attack A compound attack that deceives the opponent's simple parry.

'Open eyes' Starting a movement with no prior knowledge of how it will finish, relying on reflexes to adjust and make the correct ending.

Opposition Blade movement maintaining constant contact with the opponent's blade.

Orthopaedic grip A general term for moulded grips of various designs used on foils and épées.

Parry A defensive action to deflect an opponent's attack by opposing 'forte to opponent's foible'.

Phrase A sequence of fencing movements performed without a break.

Piste The field of play on which a bout takes place.

Pommel A metal cap screwed to the end of the blade that locks the parts of the weapon together and provides a counterbalance to the blade.

Poule (pool) The grouping of fencers or teams in a competition.

Preparation of attack The movement of blade or foot to obtain the best position from which to make an attack.

President The referee in a fencing bout.

Pressure The pressing movement of the fencer's blade against the opponent's blade, to deflect it or to cause a reaction from it.

Priority The right-of-way gained by the fencer at foil and sabre by extending the sword arm and continually threatening the opponent's target.

Pronation The position of the sword hand with the knuckles uppermost.

Rassemblement Bringing of both feet together, either forwards or backwards, so that the heels are touching with the feet at right angles and the body in an upright position.

Recovery The return to the On Guard position.

Riposte An offensive action following a successful parry of an attack.

Second-intention An action made to provoke a movement from the opponent.

Sentiment du fer The use of the tactile senses of the fingers ('feel of the blade'), mainly thumb and forefinger, to give an awareness of the blade.

Simple attack An offensive action made with one blade movement in one period of fencing time; may be direct or indirect.

Straight thrust A direct attack landing in the same line.

Successive parries Two or more consecutive parries made to defend against compound attacks.

Supination The position of the sword hand with the fingernail uppermost.

Valid hit A hit which arrives correctly on target.

Flessel-Colovic (France) v. Nagy (Hungary) in the womens épée final, Athens Olympic Games, 2004. Nagy was victorious with a 15-10 win.

FENCING CHRONOLOGY

1200 BC Evidence of fencing competitions in Egypt.

AD 476 The fall of Rome. Heavier and cruder weapons replace the short swords and light spears formerly used by soldiers.

1471 European fencing guilds, such as the Marxbruder in Germany, are organised.

1500 The first fencing manual is published. Early fencing techniques are developed in Spain around this time.

1553 The Italians begin using the rapier, and develop fencing technique.

1567 The fencing master Agrippa defines the four fencing positions – prime, seconde, tierce and quarte.

1573 The French Fencing Academy is officially recognised by King Charles IX.

1575 The French fencing master Henry de St. Didier publishes the first French fencing manual, which begins to classify many attacks and parries.

1650 The Italian masters Vigiani and Grassi describe the lunge.

1700s Rapiers decline in use and the fleuret, or foil, becomes the training weapon of choice.

1780 The right-of-way conventions are invented, making fencing much safer.

1850s The épée becomes the dueling weapon of choice in Europe. The sabre becomes the national weapon of Hungary.

1874 The fencing mask is invented by the French master La Boessiere. Italian fencing masters develop sabre fencing into a non-fatal sport. The Hungarians later develop a new school of sabre fencing and dominate the sport until the mid-20th century.

1896 The first US fencing school is founded.

1900 Men's foil and sabre competitions are included in the first modern Olympic Games.

1913 The men's épée competition is introduced at Olympic level.

1913 The Fédération Internationale d'Escrime (FIE) is founded.

1924 With the end of World War I, dueling declines in popularity. However, the sport of fencing continues to grow.

1924 The women's foil competition is introduced at Olympic level.

1936 The men's Olympic competition leads to a duel after the Italian team disagrees with the scoring of a Hungarian judge. At the Hungarian border after the Games, two duels are fought with wounds inflicted, before spectators intervene.

1950s Electric scoring for épée is introduced at Olympic level.

1954 Eastern European countries, such as the Soviet Union, Romania and Poland, begin to challenge French and Italian dominance of the sport. An Eastern European style of fencing, relying on speed and mobility, emerges.

1956 The last-known formal duel occurs in France. It ends with a scratch to the arm.

1960 Electronic scoring for foil is introduced at Olympic level.

1982 Hungarian great Aladar Gerevich wins the last of six consecutive Olympic titles. His dominance of the sabre competition runs from 1932 to 1960.

1982 Vladimir Smirnov dies at the World Championships in Rome, when a broken blade goes through his mask causing a fatal brain injury. His death prompts a review of safety standards in fencing, which leads to the development of stronger masks.

1988 Electronic scoring for sabre is introduced.

1996 Women's épée becomes an Olympic sport.

1997 Young Ho Kim loses one of the most heroic contests in World Championship history. He is down 11-3 to Sergei Golubitsky in the final period of the men's foil gold medal bout but scores 8 touches in a row to tie at 11-all before losing 15-14.

1998 Women's sabre appears in the World Championships as a demonstration sport.

2004 Women's individual sabre appears at the Athens Olympic Games.

2008 Women's team sabre is included in the programme for the Beijing Olympic Games.

INDEX